Ethereal Flowers

Primula

Ethereal Flowers

poems by

Martin Willitts, Jr.

SHANTI ARTS PUBLISHING

BRUNSWICK, MAINE

Ethereal Flowers

Published by Shanti Arts Publishing

Designed by Shanti Arts Designs

Cover and interior images are taken from early issues of *Curtis's Botanical Magazine*, which had its start in 1787. Wikimedia Commons. Public Domain.

Shanti Arts LLC
193 Hillside Road
Brunswick, Maine 04011
shantiarts.com

Printed in the United States of America

ISBN: 978-1-956056-81-5

Library of Congress Control Number: 2023933182

Contents

III. Gardening 🌱

IV.   Trees 🌿

Preface

I first studied botany as a seven-year-old child, and I learned about healing plants from my grandfather.

As an adult, I traveled from west to east on foot to rediscover some of the plants named during the Lewis and Clark Expedition because a distant ancestor knew both men. The willet, a wading bird belonging to the family of sandpipers, is named after my ancestor, Lieutenant Colonel Marinus Willett (July 31, 1740 – August 22, 1830).

Marinus Willett was the informal leader of the Sons of Liberty in New York City during the American Revolution, took part in Richard Montgomery's invasion of Canada, tried to secure help in a battle from General Benedict Arnold (at the time still an American hero), and was a judge for the spy William Butler after the war. Willett was elected to New York's Assembly. He was friendly with George Washington. His role in the French and Indian War received brief mention in the Newbery Medal-winning children's book *The Matchlock Gun*. He is also the basis for the character in *The Last of the Mohicans*. Willett's portrait by Ralph Earl (1791) is in the Metropolitan Museum of Art.

I saw the glass flowers mentioned in the first poem in the Ware Museum at Harvard University.

Acknowledgments

Gratitude is extended to the editors of these journals, magazines, anthologies, and presses that first published these poems. Like a good gardener, I am constantly weeding and pruning these poems.

Alexandria Quarterly: "Heirloom"

Black Poppy Review: "From the Closeness of Oak, Dark Holds Its Breath"

Blast Furnace: "The Bluish Butterfly Bush Calls to me"

Border Crossings: "This Is Why I Plant Perennials"

Broadkill River Review: "The Lily: The Yellow of the Columbia" and "This Typography Is Unexpected as Bitterroot"

Concis: "Osage Orange"

Ekphrastic Review: "Cup of Silver Ginger"

hotmetalpress.net: "Sunflowers"

January: "Everlasting"

languageandculture.net: "White Milkwort"

Madness Muse Press: "Snowdrops"

The Montuck Review: "Lentils"

Nine Mile Magazine: "Finding Peonies"

Parks and Points (National Parks Association): "Globe Flowers"

Poppy Road Review: "Gardening" and "Sunflowers, Sunflowers, Sunflowers"

Rattle: "Pacific Dogwood"

Raw Dog Press (postcards): "Nuttall's Toothwort"

Red Wolf Journal: "Song of Loneliness"

Shrew: "Saint Patrick's Day"

Sidereality: "Edible Thistle" and "Four-Winged Saltbush"

Verse-Virtual: "Blue Elderberry"; "Broom Snakeweed"; "Mad Dog Plant"; "Purple Wake-Robin"; "Salmonberry"; and "Tansy"

Wilderness House Literary Review: "Bloodroot"; "Dutchman's Breeches"; and "Trillium"

Writer's Monthly: "Lacy Tansyaster"; "Lemon Scurfpea"; "Long-Leaved Mugwort"; "Maiden Blue-Eyed Mary"; and "Mountain Balm"

"Thirteen Ways to Digest a Purple Coneflower" was part of a mini-chapbook by the same title, Origami Poetry Project, 2013

"Calendula" appeared in Writer Rising Up, 2014 Digging to the Roots Calendar, Month of October

"Canyon Gooseberry"; "Shrubby Beardtongue"; "Texas Bluebonnet"; and "Thimbleberry" appeared in *The Restlessness of the Gardener,* a poetry mini-chapbook by Origami Poetry Project, 2016

"Communion with the Trees" appeared in the anthology *Weatherings,* FutureCycle Press, 2015

"Companion Planting" appeared in *Some Things You Can Never Repair,* Black Poppy chaplet

"Daffodils" won the 2014 International Dylan Thomas Poetry Award, a one-time award in honor of the Centennial of Dylan Thomas's birth

"Daffodils" appears in *Dylan Thomas and the Writing Shed,* FutureCycle Press, 2017

"Druid Astrology is Written in the Trees" appeared in the anthology about astrology *What's Your Sign,* A Kind of Hurricane Press, 2013

"Ethereal Flowers" was part of the anthology *Pandemic Diaries,* Poemeleon, 2020

"Irises, Irises" won the *Big River Review* Poem of the Month award, June 2012

"Milkweed" was a Featured Entry in the International Hour of Writes contest

"The Sunflower" appeared in the anthology *Like Light: 25 Years of Poetry and Prose,* Bright Hill Press, 2018

"Tenderness" originally appeared as "Touch Is Something We All Need" in the anthology *In Terra Place,* Cinnamon Press, 2011

Lily

Ethereal Flowers

One of Harvard's most famous treasures is the internationally acclaimed
Ware Collection of Blaschka Glass Models of Plants, the *Glass Flowers*.
This unique collection of over 4,300 models, representing more than 780
plant species, was created by glass artisans Leopold and Rudolf Blaschka, a
father and son team of Czech glass artists.

These delicate glass flowers, complete with stem and veined leaf,
stop me into silence, make me consider how they were created
with pieces resembling so many different plants,
some of which I've never seen. Each small section
is supported by tiny, almost unnoticeable wires,
all subtly holding color and light.

Every bud opens like a person waiting for a first kiss.
Apple blossoms; yellow leopard-spotted tiger lilies;
parts of a cashew tree; a cactus waving hello with one arm
offering a pink flower—every miniature stigma, anther,
and filament of the pistil was fashioned from sand,
soda ash and limestone, heated into a liquid, molten glass
blown fluid becoming flowers in a breeze from Harvard Square.

Narcissus

I.

Healing Plants

Sunflowers, Sunflowers, Sunflowers

Based on Vincent van Gogh's sunflower paintings; sunflowers
(*Helianthus annuus*) draw toxins out of the ground

I carry armfuls of sunflowers into my room,
scatter them across my yellow bed,
plow deep into them,
tossing them as poems the thickness of paint.
Some enter into my skin—

love is here! love is here! love is here!

Finding Peonies

Tree peony (*Paeonia suffruticosa*); used as an antioxidant,
antitumor, antipathogenic, immune modulating agent, and
protector of the cardiovascular and central nervous systems

Peonies at dusk: I know the world will be alright.
In spite of all the cruelty in the world, regardless of words
rendering us less than we are, no matter the wrongness
done to each other and the land, there are peonies
finding light at the latest part of the day. When the sun
does not know enough to stand still and admire
what is opening, and what is dying, and what finds loss
and what finds a reason to continue anyway, there are peonies
so in tune with love that they practically tug at my heart.

I return home with a basket of green oranges I intend to ripen.
Some still have a stem and leaf attached, refusing to let go.
We all have to age and let go someday. My skin is already
wrinkled and puckered as a rind; however, my ambitions
are still as green as a teen. The wooden basket with wire handles
is as old as my memory of orange crates, using one
to stand on in a town square to shout against the war.
The crate could hold my weight then, but it would snap now.

The moon is orange outside. It will be unseasonable hot.
Looking at my basket will not make the fruit ripen faster.
Impatience has always been my strong suit. Imagine, if you will,
what might be my weakness, and you will not be any closer.
I leave the peonies outside where time has its own meaning.

❧

I am beginning to think I have a hand-me-down life.
I have already out-lived so many people. I am losing count
how many I still know, and how many are beginning to forget
who they are. Life is not a contest to see who lives the longest.

It should be a contest of who loves the best with intensity.
Who could say what will become of me?

When I die, I can say I looked so long at a peony
I memorized it. I stare until well past bedtime, until I forgot
what time it is. And it is a different kind of forgetful;
not the kind where everything I know ceases to exist.

When I die, I shall say I ate oranges
until my skin became their color, spitting pips
like we used to with watermelon seeds, seeing how far
they could go in an arc, trying for distance, getting a mess.

When I die, I shall say I never really grew up. It will be
an important fact, one to get me into some good graces.
I could hang my hat on that if I ever wore a hat.

I want to live my life as if it was acid-free paper.

❦

Things might have ended differently. I might not have
put on my shoes with the right heel lift, and a drone
might not have been launched at a distance.
I might not have gotten dressed for a walk,
and some politician might have declared war
although he had no authority to do so.
I might not have found my way to the woods
to get away from the insanity where *no* means *yes*,
and someone might have noticed the leaking toxins
before they entered the only source of drinkable water.

I might not have bought oranges before hiking,
thinking I would take one with me, but they were green.
So, I left them in the house, and someone shot school kids.

If I had watched the news like a basset hound, nose
trying to bury sadness, I might not have seen the peonies.

Some say there is no such concept as coincidence—
every occurrence has a plan even if we do not see it.
Today, I saw peonies, and my heart was healed for a moment.

❧

I would like to say I found the peonies because I needed them.
I would like to say the peonies found *me*—
the moment was ripe for it. I would like to say the oranges
were fresh as a promise no one intends to keep.

The simple fact is that I went for a walk, bought
oranges out of season, took them home anyway
too ashamed to put them back, went out
for no reason, and wandered around like a stray animal.
My mind went blank, numb, and the next I knew
I was in the woods, startled into awakening,
and there were white peonies, so natural
and so unobtrusive. It was later than I thought,
so I headed back because I did not want to get lost
in the dark directionless. There were no plans.
Sometimes, no plans are the best ones.

When I find peonies at dusk, the world is alright.

Daffodils

(Narcissus pseudonarcissus)

A daffodil bud is seen among the snow,
offering forgiveness. Winter was harsh,
and the brutality of summer is not far away.
We need forgiveness. Surely, after tribulations
there is relief. Already we are gardening dreams.
It had been huddling like an old gray woman
grabbing her shawl, in an underground house,
stirring a promise to return.
Soon its six petals harmonic sense will bring love.

All day, it radiates. Although it has not grown,
you can feel the end of winter, like curtains rustling.
It appeared in the Garden of Gethsemane as relief,
and felt what would happen next. It was also there
for the Roman soldiers who bit its bulb to ease
their wounds, knowing what would happen next.

Now it's here for us, and we do not know what will happen.
We only see so far, and things go pass faster. Tolerance
is easier as we become older, and suffering becomes normal
as our bodies find new ailments. In our dreams we plant.
We are yellow petals caught in a frayed shawl.

In a world uncertain what will happen next,
there are some things we can expect and some we can't.
The snow understands it cannot stand in the daffodil's way.

Blue Elderberry

(Sambucus glauca)

bluish-black
excellent in jelly
sky drooling from my mouth
I see blueness
quite pleasant

although red elder is toxic

Native Americans use this plant
to treat sore or swollen limbs
headaches and relief from pain and swelling
and antiseptic washes

I could wash away the world with these berries
all my aches would ebb
my breath would be blue jays and hollyhocks

come closer and observe

Broom Snakeweed

(Gutierrezia sarothrae)

a type of sunflower snakes
a fleck of yellow in your iris
they almost disappear between two fingers

if you boil twenty-five grams of the petal
in a liter of water
drink its yellow one to three times a day

you will sweat out impurities
your stomach pains will dissipate into yellow rain
your lungs will clear the clouds of bronchitis

pneumonia will drizzle until forgotten
a grin will sweep clean
your rain-streaked face

Milkweed

(*Asclepias syriaca*); a folk medicine for kidney problems

All rain-drenches spring through lonely summer, I wait.
I wait like a Buddhist, like a sparrow waiting for worms
to float to the surface after a torrential rain.

Patience, my heart and mind, do not be jumpy monarchs
in an endless open field of white milkweed—wait!

All through high temperatures, I wait
like a drill sergeant scanning new-meat recruits
to determine if he could whip them into shape,
only to be fodder for gunfire.

I count the few individual raindrops during this transition,
waiting, while black crickets rub their legs into music,
like seasons grinding knives. Not once does that bulb open.

In one of my moments of weakness—
a bathroom break from bloated kidney,
or chasing the black feral cat away from the birdfeeder
where it is practicing silence and meditation
to encourage a sparrow to fall into its path—
the milkweed opens its surprised mouth and releases,

tiny spores go crazy indirect directions, released
as men who die in far-off lands
waiting for their end to come and taking too long to die.
The milkweed drift into that merging.

The milkweed spores do not question, nor ask
the purpose of life—they simply surrender.

Thirteen Ways to Digest a Purple Coneflower

Echinacea (*Echinacea purpurea*); used as a cure for colds, pain
and inflammation, urinary tract infections, chronic fatigue
syndrome, attention-deficit/hyperactivity disorder, influenza,
bee stings, allergies, hay fever, and eczema.

1

a seed in a packet knows its solemn truth
without reading its promise

already it is dreaming

2

healing coneflower
silence a cold
do what you do best

a purple sun rises

3

an inflamed wind inhales coneflowers
and feels better all week

tell the earth the good news:
a repair for fatigue
is on the way

4

what a doctor does not know
can cure you

the coneflower winks its red eye
your nightmares are almost over
sparrows chatter like raindrops
about infinite possibilities

the garden hoe already unearths them

5

thirteen coneflowers talk among themselves
in total agreement

what looks like a conspiracy
is an attachment
to the thing dreams are made of

thirteen heads bob mutely
needing nothing more to be said
one way
or the other

6

the coneflower aspires
to match the picture on the seed packet
and more

no imperfections
rising to the occasion
and not to be the occasional

7

it rains coneflowers
just when the dry ground is thirsty

8

count coneflowers
from the pulse of the earth
a woman's moans
in the lost wind
of thirteen promises
winking
into nothingness

9

a coneflower grows out a saxophone
purple notes of loss
raining seed packets
where some seeds might fail
never amount to anything

but the ones
reaching the high notes

these
are the ones
worth smelling

10

a sparrow lands on a coneflower
and takes off when it bends
never sees it straighten itself
calling *come back come back*
sing to me

11

if we turn it into a tincture
the coneflower could heal
what is wrong
between us

over distances
where winds never return

12

we pour pitchers of pictures
of coneflowers
into wings of wind
into heart-shaped suns
into imperfect agreements
into healing
we can only dream about

13

the thirteen sax notes are notations
of what to do

a sparrow without a song
is a wind without a song
is a song without coneflowers

are packets of seed
our heart needs for healing

are thirteen promises
for repairing distances
great and small

Do Not Be Stilled, My Heart

Based on Vincent van Gogh's painting of Dr. Gachet, *Portrait of Dr. Gachet* (1890), who is shown with a branch of foxglove

Foxglove (*Digitalis purpurea*) is used to treat irregular heartbeat, including atrial fibrillation and "flutter"; asthma; epilepsy; tuberculosis; constipation; headache; and spasm. Van Gogh may have been under the influence of digitalis intoxication, the side effects of which are xanthopsia and coronas.

Do not be still, my heart—
days are sunflowers.

Do not stay still, my lungs—
auras are dark church naves,
angels in crossroads carry fresh bread.

I am beyond tired—shutters close.
Prayers spawn in air.

I begin with a heart, grounded
into powder.
I need another day, and another,
strung into prayer beads.

When the possibility of rain is questionable,
calm is just at the edge of air
clapping leaves in a slow breeze.

Purple Wake-Robin

Purple trillium or stinking Benjamin (*Trillium petrolatum*)

a solitary flower
with an unpleasant odor rising
above a whorl of three broadly ovate
diamond-shaped leaves

petals are maroon
sepals green as a robin's song waking

the fruit is oval
a reddish berry
I inspect with robin's eyes

herbalists use this ill-scented plant
to cure gangrene
since they believe
plants are used to alleviate
the ailments they resemble

like the robin's nest between your legs
the diamond-shaped leaves I open
the maroon seed between my fingers
your eyes become
the purple screams of birds in flight

I am not solitary again
because you are awake

Lentils

(Lens culinaris); self-pollinating and are a good food for diabetics

Yellow lentils are boiled as the first food
for the Ethiopian baby. My Shia friend says,
lentils are blessed by seventy prophets. Holy is the name
of the first to meet the sunrise and the last to see sunset.
Today, I am the first to rise. This is what comes,
what goes, what is endless, what must never end.

My Italian neighbor is picking lentils.
He says the round coin-like shape is considered good-luck:
the beginning of a prosperous new year.
He is so rich he shares with his neighbors.
He does this until sunset, stars falling as lentils,
blessings from seventy prophets.

Calendula

(*Calendula arvensis*); represents October and is used in treating wounds

On the *Day of the Dead*, the sun is bleeding,
and I have this incredible cure
in these clock-shaped yellow flower petals.
I could save so many wounds by the time you wake,
but the foretelling of winter is not one of them.
The spirits can rise, and they can fall in the Fall
rush during deadness of leaves. We can only digest so much,
but the news is not one of them. Even now,
someone is denying science or ancient herbs.
I have seen where marigolds protect tomatoes,
yet people look incredulously at me. They say,
global warming is not the sign of the *End of Times*,
while praying for doomsday, counting the days
like these petals. Tomorrow, this day of the dead
will be over, the calendula will wither, the sun will tilt,
and we will not digest the coming of age, our hearts
ticking slow as a snow shower. They will say,
nothing is happening; it is all temporary. Already,
the trees toss bouquets of yellow leaves,
already forming buds for the next revival.

"Mad Dog Plant"

Plains coneflower, pani, or pawnee corn (*Echinacea angustifolia*); planted
eight times among the fruit trees in Thomas Jefferson's south orchard;
"highly prized by the natives as an efficacious remedy in the cure of the bite
of the rattlesnake, or mad dog." —Thomas Jefferson

a dwarf corn
only twenty-four inches high
is bred for the harshness
of the short northern Plains growing season

they ripen quickly six weeks from planting

small and vivacious
like his wife in the garden
her hands turning dirt

Jefferson could feel pain lessening
abating after the snake bit

a tickle of yellow
shaking rattle soft
as a kiss

The Sunflower

(*Helianthus annuus*); removes negative toxicity from the ground,
then you toss the flowers; otherwise, you can eat the seeds just
like birds and squirrels do

opens its green fist
one finger at a time
until we witness
all the yellow triangles
surrounding the large brown button of seeds

it remains attentive to the sun for weeks
then slowly curls its yellow triangles
dropping one by one
until all that remains
is the brown center
being eaten by small birds

I am glancing at pictures of my son
transitioning from infant to adult

I could not see either while they happened
transpiring and conspiring to make me older
under the surface of forever

I am at the summit of time
descending
while the matte finish of my son ascends

I can tell you this

the incline is somehow more straight down vertical

I do not want to let go just yet
any more than that last yellow petal does

Yarrow

Nosebleed plant, carpenter's root, old man's pepper, soldier's woundwort
(*Achillea millefolium*); used as a cure for inflammation, colds, nosebleeds,
circulation problems, menstrual cramps, high blood pressure, bleeding

Achilles carried yarrow into battle to heal the soldiers;
I plan to cure a lot of people with this *carpenter's root*,
hammering broken worlds into whole.
I combine its blue oils with peppermint to cure influenza.
I inhale it to cure my asthma.
I lay on a sachet of yarrow and dream of my lover.
My loss is repaired, and now I want to fix everything.

I want to doctor the earth itself. I can hear its grief.
I wish I could use the leaves
for nosebleed in the sky.
I would use the aerial parts
to stimulate the high blood pressure of the fields.

I would use it to alleviate
the years of abuse the land has withstood.
I would tilt the earth's wounded lips
and drizzle juices through parched openings.
Toxins would be released like a broken fever.

When I say, *Drink three cups of Yarrow's tea until well,*
people will open their eyes from the fog of battle
and see that a starling has made its nest in yarrow.
The hole in the universe will become repaired.

Irises, Irises

(Iris germanica); based on Vincent van Gogh's painting *Irises* (1889)

Irises, irises, absorb lightning around me,
draw it into yourself, into your blue arms,
a tension-storm hovering over our horizon,
painting everything with pain. Relieve me.
Spare me. Your blue words are in my fingers.
You are a woman with delicate hearing,
knowing my suffering is seasonal. Listen,
the dawn is blue as illness, and no one listens.
Irises, irises, absorb the lightning out of me.
I do not understand the world and its lack of flowers.

Where I am staying is shut off from the noise,
but the noise is moaning from the pores of the walls
with incredible pain. Life is wood-blocks of loss.
Irises, irises, absorb the lightning towards me,
hold my breath in your sad blue arms.
I want to be in the unusual angle of love.
There is no fall of light when you are away.
Irises, irises, you are a woman that never stays.
Drag me out into sunlight; fill my day with blue rain;
pull out the agony; and fill my pond with lilies.

Return to me. Drench me in blueness.
Become quick washes of heartbeats in terminal clouds.
Be an asylum from hurt and shame. Heal me.
Irises, irises, strike everything with blue lightning.
You are a study of air and life, of a lonely countryside,
a woman neither here nor there, fragile as my heart
when you are gone. Your petals of words on the floor
whisper, *I am here for you, I am here for you.*
Irises, irises, your words are blue lightning surrounding me.
The odor sizzles in air, painting a landscape with love.

Sunflowers

Based on Vincent van Gogh's painting *Sunflowers* (1887),
made to show Cezanne

I want to decorate my room with color
from sunflowers of all I can imagine
sharing the arbitrary orange and yellow
I selected from the field of my imagination

placed them on a table
so that it's the first and last thing one sees
when entering or leaving in a hurry
compelling a person to slow down

enjoy the released yellow envelopes
from a distance I have not opened

I want to express myself
but I dare not
less my enthusiasm overwhelms you
and my words open as sunflowers

no one should see so much yellow

I hold back
afraid of having so much love
it makes your cheeks turn orange

stay a while
paint with me
let our paintings sigh
let the rooms be yellow mornings

Snowdrops

(Galanthus nivalis); used to treat Alzheimer's disease

The harsh winter is over.
These first spring flowers are here,
just when all hope seems lost.
I have almost forgotten what I was about to do—
the news is so unsettling,
days blending into a daze.
These small, white drooping bells never ring
warning when we disremember what is important.
We miss so much when we lose focus.

The flowers arrive like doctors in white lab coats,
testing my short-term memory.
What's the last thing you remember?

It's not important to remember the date anymore,
let alone when I returned from a tour of Vietnam,
arriving in winter, I think, when snow
was waning. Or maybe snow was still in the air.
I'm not certain. I was limping, if I recall,
from my burn wounds I treated with aloe.
The news was disturbing then, too.
I distinctly heard church bells chiming.

But I recall snowdrops, where snow melted,
after I returned, and I knew I was home.
Everything else is certain.

Terminal

Cezanne, the sunflowers are dying.
They have been waiting for you to see them.
They repeat your name.
Fishermen find your name in their nets.
The sunflowers are damaged by this calling.
I tried painting them into walls, into the café
where I write letters to my brother about this loss.
The streets wash away in rain.
The sunflowers' petals fall, one tragedy after another.
No one can stop the decline. It is exasperating.
Ruin, it all turns to ruin.
I am waiting for you to open the door.
If there is only one thing I can understand, it is voices
no one hears. If there are somethings I cannot comprehend,
they are the absence of days, the routes of the untraveled heart,
the passing of sunflowers, the feeling
things are slipping,
the silence in your letter that never arrives.

I have to ask: *Is there something wrong with me?*

8070

Lady's Slipper

II.

Plants Discovered During the Lewis and Clark Expedition

Rocky Mountain Bee Plant

(*Cleome serrulata*); used for stomach aches, fevers, and as a dye

the wildness of flowers swarming
leaflets sting from one point
at end of its leaf stalk
hexagon-shaped like bees' wax

the inflorescence arises
when vegetative growth
subsequently resumes
from stem apex
terminal as the hive in smoke
final as the colony
when the queen does not emerge

pink or reddish-purple flowers
the urge to fly

flowers produce copious nectar
attracting bees
bees by the hoards

in times of drought
early Spanish-Americans
made tortillas
from the barely palatable
but nourishing seeds
I break the seeds
like bees
between my fingers

Edible Thistle

(*Cirsium edule*)

how incongruous a thistle
that can be eaten when boiled
and tastes delightful

a wooly mass of astonishment
with many spines forming pedestals
several rose-purple petals

found at high altitudes
elating towards our hunger
boiling towards our surprise

Four-Wing Saltbush

(Atriplex canescens)

four paper-like wings
project from the seed at right angles
in alkaline soil habitats

white leaves
shaped like a goose's foot
waddling between pinyon-juniper

the seeds were cooked like oatmeal
ground-up seeds were mixed with sugar and water
for a drink called Pinole

sometimes they were used as a leavening ingredient
for breads or
used in making lye to soften the hulls of corn

paper thin
leaves
honk and rise

Thimbleberry

(Rubus perviflorus)

a small flowered bramble briar
scrambling showy white flowers
resistant to
and generally enhanced by fire

the bark was boiled made into soap
leaves were used to make a medicinal tea
young shoots may be eaten as greens

so small
so fiery
just a thimble

This Topography Is Unexpected as Bitterroot

(*Lewisia rediviva*); state flower of Montana

1

bitterroot can live for more than a year without water

its pink blossoms conspire close to the ground
it can hear itself called the "resurrection flower"

bitterroot can be dried and pressed
then revived after being soaked

you can eat its roots but seldom raw

it tastes bitter
its resultant swelling
causes great discomfort like childbirth

Native American women boiled the root
mixing with meat or berries
pulverizing and seasoning it
with deer fat and moss
molded into patties
carried on hunting expeditions
or war parties

2

press this flower between pages
press it between your lips
pretend it is me after the lost time
revive me with your lips

3

get close to the ground

listen

the roots speak of bitter years
the pink sunrise is pulverized in the raw

buffalo rustle as petticoats

I clamp tight this page
and soak it with the missing

the thirst is immediate and distant

The Lilly: The Yellow of the Columbia

(Fritillaria pudica)

it grows throughout the Pacific northwest
in well-drained and dry
sunny sites and is today
a valued rock garden species
for its nodding
golden-yellow flowers and its petite habit

it reminded Jefferson of his wife's hand
and her smell

it defied reason

it swelled with the seasons

it haunted him at candlelight
like his wife
in the oval cameo and in the oval
of a bed

Western Springbeauty

(*Claytonia lanceolata*)

from the foothills
and uncovered mountain slopes
to alpine meadows
just below snow banks

a small
delicate perennial
five pinkish-white petals
with dark veins

the flower has two green sepals
below the petals and five
bright pink stamens
a pair of lance-shaped leaves

when boiled they have the taste and texture
of baked potatoes

Native Americans dug these in early spring
when snow melted like butter

Lacy Tansyaster

(*Machaeranthera pinnatifida*); also known as yellow spiny daisy

a slender plant with small
weakly bristly leaves
one yellow flower head
at tip of each of many upper branches

these are my fingertips
these are the days that were ashamed
these were the excuses so weak
so bristly you wanted nothing to do with them

I branch out and you ignore
you bristle in the kitchen clanging pots
making yellow noises and tipping glasses
your voice is slender and sadden

Salmonberry

(*Rubus spectabilis*); also known as cloudberry,
yellowberry, and baked apple berry

oh spawn on my tongue
oh leap in my streams
go against the current
defy gravity
follow ambition & drive

flow tart
eat out of hand

swim in preserves and liqueurs
I can go crazy drunk with you

be a yellow cloud

be light-orange when young
be what I cannot be

salmon eggs

Lemon Scurfpea

(Psoralidium lanceolatum)

longing for dry sandy areaselongated thin stalks
with ovate leaves
cluster their small purplish-white flowers
like a chicken gathers its chicks under wing

it wants the shifting sand
it wants sand dunes the size of henhouses

it wants grains of sand as special as chicks
purple tongues begging for shelter

it cares little for a grain of rain

if you open an egg
notice the lemon color

it speaks of sand and safe wings
it reminds you that you too crave a safe place
it is a grain of sand you need

Long-Leaved Mugwort

(*Artemisia longifolia*)

I can recite your name all day
the shrub of your surname reverts
it back into the soil
it thunders
it is rich as topsoil
it is strange as impatience

when I repeat your name
owls awaken

in the silence
I wonder what I have done
the universe is disturbed and hunted

in the space of five minutes
talons clutch
dirt is shifted and wet leaves tremble
eyes narrow and focus
the mice long regret this calling

Mountain Balm

(Ceanothus velutinus); also known as sticky laurel,
tobacco brush, snowbrush, and buckbush

posed on the ledge
I give it so many possible names

clusters open fragrant as fresh bread
creamy-white flowers

contrasted
with dark balsam-scented host of sweets

the sticky foliage
this broadleaf evergreen shrub

the snowbrush's stems
stout as a baker

much-branched
lending spreading

round-topped
like frosting on a cake

so many choices
impossible to choose

Mountain Lady's Slipper

(*Cypripedium montanum*)

these orchids grow in Montana
yellow or white and delicate
as a lady's slipper and
the crown of petals above
a deep
subdued purple

slightly twisted
like a Sultan harems' slippers

they hang down like purple ribbons
as ballerina straps

these orchids prefer more sunlight
and less water
than their Calypso cousins do

as airy as a garden walk in open toed sandals

as rare as a pair of comfortable shoes
and should not be picked
or dug up or kicked loose by a high heel

they are sneakers on thick carpets

thousands of seeds are contained
within an erect
elliptical
hairy capsule
pushed together like a Japanese woman's toes
in forceful excruciating shoes

Sugarbowls

(*Clematis hirsutissima*); also known as hairy clematis, leather flower, vase flower, and lion's beard

small
inverted urns
each stem
purplish-brown or
dull reddish lavender
or dull violet

a hirsute plant
with several stems
in a dense clump
like a stack of teacups

sepals flare outward
and give the flower
a "sugar bowl" appearance

all I need is a spoon
a whistle of tea
the reddish glow of my wife

her one eyebrow raised
small and polite
demure and expressive
when sipping me
like a teacup

it is enough to boil me over

White Milkwort

(Polygala alba); much milk lactates from nipple
of white bilaterally symmetrical flowers

slender erect stems
responds narrowly
in cone-shaped expression

the fields are abundant
thrashing in the aftermath of wind
exhausted

sated for now
only for now

Canyon Gooseberry

(Ribes menziescii)

their leaves tend to be smaller
less resinous
or sticky

the stems have three spines per node
often the fruits are covered with glandular hairs
and spines

unremarkable for their edibility
jewel-like flowers in early spring
particularly lovely at close range

their maroon eyes study us
the redwood forest moves in closer
making us as small as the berry

Shrubby Beardtongue

(*Penstemon fruticosus*); also known as shrubby penstemon

a bushy plant
usually much broader than tall
with large showy
pale lavender
or pale blue-violet
bilaterally
symmetrical flowers
in crowded
narrow clusters at stem ends

tenement complexes
a city outgrowing itself

a broad lavender
conversation
with the tongue
of unbuttered bread

Texas Bluebonnet

(*Lupinus texensis*); the "flowering pea of the plains
of Arkansas" —Thomas Jefferson

in the Monticello oval flower bed in April 1807
one seed was saved by Jefferson's granddaughter
Anne Randolph

Jefferson alleged
it was "remarkable for its beautiful blossom & leaf"
yet later relegated it to his south orchard

the identity of this flowering pea is still a puzzle

traditionally
Monticello gardeners have interpreted "Lewis' pea"
as highly ornamental

if that one seed could speak
would it say

we are transplanted dreams
the rain on dry grass
the wash of paintbrushes whispering the sunrise
the night and the restlessness of the gardener
seeking the compelling blend of surprise
even if for a moment
reflecting the pale autumn sky

Osage Orange

(Maclura pomifera); a tree species native to the
southern Mississippi valley

one Osage bow was worth
a horse and blanket in trade

it has convoluted grapefruit-sized fruit
on the female trees

formidable thorns on young shoots
yellow-colored bark

its lush foliage
was sheared effectively into impenetrable hedges

the invention of barbed wire
soon made Osage orange hedges less desirable

Maiden Blue-Eyed Mary

(Collinsia parviflora)

on open gravelly flats
and river banks
small
widely branching plants
with tiny blue-and-white flowers
symmetrical
on slender stalks
smaller than her blue eyes

my Mary's lips are so blue
parting
as the tiniest of flowers
in sunlight
her arms encasing me in welcome

my voice is so much gravel
when I tell her
the banks of her cheeks
sob petite round flowers

Iris

III.

Gardening

Gardening

It is getting warmer, so I remove my jacket.
I keep digging in the same area to plant vegetables.

No matter how many times I pitchfork
and deep-shovel, I find surprises that don't belong:

this year, a spoon; a silver key, bent askew;
a box cutter; a zippo lighter; a rubber drain stopper.

I sift dirt through a strainer and find a dime.
I was searching for worms. I find leaves I mulched;

several rocks of different sizes; a tree root, wide as a fist;
half a walnut shell the squirrel hid for later.

I can testify to the strength of the sudden gust.
It flaps around my spring coat as I chase it.

It took away the mourning dove's song from its throat
clear over the garage into a neighbor's yard.

Companion Planting

Every year, our small garden is crowded by my over planning.
I forget how wide the yellow squash leaves fan out,
and now they are shading the onions. My enthusiasm creates
fifteen-foot snow peas, butternuts crawling over the asphalt,
more loose-leaf lettuce than a rabbit can eat.

Someday, my planting and harvesting will end. The weeds
will take back what is theirs. The feral will sniff out
of darkness. There will be nothing left of me except mulch.

But who is to say if a woman might bring pruning gloves,
her hair tied under a bandana? She might bend over the earth,
trowel in her hand, green eyes focused on the hole she has dug.
She could plant a tomato and pat the ground around it, talking to it.
She might slide her finger on the furry underside
just to smell tomato on her fingers.

This Is Why I Plant Perennials

Every time I plant the perennials—
daffodils, tulips, tiger lilies, delphiniums—
I'm leaving a part of me immortal:
my immeasurable desire.

I anticipate those first green shoots,
foreshadowing my promise to myself.
Planting is more than peaceful,
silent meditation, or renewal.

When perennial flowers die, falling to darkness,
they will not represent eventual revival
or the promise of return, yet their roots
are reminders of my pledges for more.

More voices, more colors, more for
someone to remember me. People
might see them and comment,
I saw him planting there—

flowers forever arriving on schedule:
daffodils, pink tulips, tiger lilies tasting
sunlight, four-foot delphiniums
standing against the weathered fence.

Heirloom

An heirloom is any seed saved and reused over a period of years. Feverfew (*Tanacetum parthenium*) is a healing plant for fevers. Peace vine cherry tomatoes (*Solanum lycopersicum*) have the highest amino acid count, and brandywine is a large, sweet tomato that easily cracks.

What appears renewed—the feverfew
are close to the ground, laid out as doilies—
seems only to result in ruin: black seed casings,
rubbed between my fingers, crunch, fall
to spread, seeds making white daisies
with egg-yolk-yellow centers. What appears
to be death leads towards renewal, wanting
their turn, contemplating the next chapter.

We cannot do this returning. I envy seeds.
I recycle tomato seeds of peace vine cherry
and baseball sized Brandywine.
I plant inside during March these starter seeds
in peat pots; rub their fuzzy stalks, smelling
tomatoes; plant; harvest; save seeds for winter.

Tansy

A mint; its Greek root meaning is immortality

Many of us might wish to live longer.
This is why the Greeks told stories about immortality.

Smelling this mint might make us want to live forever
in never-ending greenness.

We might want to live as long as glaciers or permafrost
but would live longer than our great-great-grandchildren.

Time scurries like ants. We live in contrary desires.
Maybe this is why we are short-lived and foolish.

Maybe we are supposed to notice how clouds move
as dirigibles, how leaves unmoor from branches,

how life is short as snowflakes. Mint reminds us
immortality is a forbidden fruit like holly berries.

None of us can live forever. We can only know
the impossible in order to dream differently.

Saint Patrick's Day

Shamrock (*Trifolium dubium*)

As a child, I used to hunt for four leaf clovers. I never knew a true shamrock would have a yellow flower with three leaves.

The Irish ate that clover during times of famine, preferring it to starvation. We never know what we will do in times of hardship until it arrives for us.

The shamrock was part of regenerative powers of nature. I believed if I found one, I could bring it to my dying Irish grandmother, and all would be well. One bite and the odor of death in her mouth would be replaced by sweetness. Even as a child, I knew the old ways of healing plants.

Grandmother said the three leaves represented the Trinity. Three is a magic number of the pyramid. It is the number of visiting kings in Matthew. It is the tripod for a telescope. It is the three kisses over a pot to bring luck to a meal. Three times the rooster called before Peter realized his error, and it was too late to take back his ill-chosen denials.

As a member of the Ancient Order of Hibernians, grandmother would see the shamrock and recall the day before she left Ireland; this would help her get well when all else failed.

Little did I understand that death comes for all of us.

Observations

Japanese anemones on the border of a shady walkway know what to do when it gets too hot: find shade. They close, shaking their fists. In appreciation of nice weather, their pinkish-mauve flowers on goldish stamens wave like hands with five webbed fingers. In tai chi, this is called *Clouds for Hands*.

❧

The young wife may be plotting against her much older, extremely-rich husband. I notice the dark, reddish-purple flowers of the poisonous monkshood in her yard.

❧

A neighbor uses a ruler to measure the hole to make sure it was nine inches deep. He fills it with sandy soil and humus. Then, he places a purple-brown bulb in the hole. He faithfully waters his speciosum lily all spring. Even when it rains, he uses his watering can.

Late August, there are the lily's large pendulant pinkish-white flowers with crimson spots, tiny as fire ants. The fragrance could be smelled for blocks away. Bees came for miles like heavy traffic.

Patience is sometimes rewarded. We just have to have enough serenity to not be disappointed with failure.

❧

The blotched white and yellow flowers of the black locust tree angle towards the earth. Maybe God is fishing for healers. This bark can be distilled to help someone to purge.

Look for flowering current. If we bruise the heart-shaped rosy-pink and white flowers, their smell will make the room calm.

In the garden, the impatiens offers a cure for bee stings and poison ivy.

This coniferous brush is springy and has reddish-brown sapwood which was once used to make long bows for the Battle of Agincourt. It is usually found near church cemeteries, and it is associated with sadness.

Yews can live for thousands of years. Norse mythology suggests a yew was the World Tree where Odin sacrificed his eye so he could foresee the future all the way to the end of the world.

Some religions substitute yew leaves for palms on Good Friday, a time that began as a feast and a celebration of Passover, but turned darkly within a week.

Cup of Silver Ginger

(Zingiber officinale); based on painting by Georgia O'Keeffe (1939)

The lime-green in the center on this plant
draws into an enigmatic forest
of a Hawaiian island
where we find what we've never seen
yet experience
it now happening. This sensuous opening
of pink and white flowers,
protects us from spirits.

Georgia peels open a gateway,
trying to have us focus
on the close-up details, like a camera,
like a woman knowing
the world can be welcoming—a ritual
for healing, and offers the cure.

She wants us to take this cup and drink it,
take our pain like communion,
open whatever closed us off from each other,
present this image
that can take away our concerns.

She does not walk gingerly
but thrusts forward
the only world she believes in.

Take this cup, she offers generously,
in remembrance of me.

Globe Flowers

(Trollius acaulis); also known as trollis

below western mountain ranges
lilac-colored globes curve for attention
cupped like hands testing spring rain

umbrellas turn the wrong way by wind
whispers of sprinkles
light as a cat's footsteps stalking a bird

after the prevailing storm
I hold your hand
yellow offerings from wet heavy clay earth

I do not feel this world spinning
but I know it does
like those merry-go-round globe flowers

if I had one story to spin
you would be in it
cupped in my hands

Everlasting

The *everlasting* is a vague promise of what will happen
beyond this life, this path of green and water and light.

Every year, I enjoy the spring purple violets,
the quizzical bees following memory, the rapture
of Cataula's one-week white flower, the scarlet cardinals,
the breathlessness of yellow tanagers that never return
again, the untouched grotto with pure water, the singing
of a child on the other side of a fence.

A Corner of the Garden of
St. Paul's Hospital at St. Rémy

Based on *A Corner of the Garden of St. Paul's Hospital at St Rémy* (1889),
a drawing by Vincent van Gogh

Irises twist their hands.
Van Gogh's afraid to leave his room. It is too much
to watch their torment.
The doctors try to calm him,
but their words do not work anymore.
The irises' energy sag.
They do not sleep any more soundly than he does.
The irises' mouths slacken.
They are cornered.

All he wants to do is leave. Being outside
does not help. He feels enclosed.
The doctors cannot help him at all.
Doctors' words cannot calm him or anyone.
There are only so many things to be said,
only so many windows to open.

The world closes in with a locked door.

Prescription

Based on *The Red Vineyard* (1888) by Vincent van Gogh,
the only painting he ever sold

Women are picking grapes of words
in the redness of late, hot day, when the river
carries messages of childbirth pain nearby.
The sense of place is senseless,
and their spines curve with drudgery
just to crush the meanings into poetry or wine.
The geography of suffering is imprinted in the wine,
a reminder of what should be.
The precise conditions of the vineyard are regulated
like a sonnet. The women suffer in the unbearable meter
of the burgundy sun.

Van Gogh does not taste this misery.
The worse the soil, the better the wine.
This is the depravation of harvesters
working near Arles, where he lives.
He felt their bruised thumbs on his forehead:
"Every day I take the remedy
that the incomparable Dickens prescribes against suicide.
It consists of a glass of wine, a piece of bread with cheese,
and a pipe of tobacco." If there is comfort in that glass,
knowing how those women toil endlessly, he cannot taste it.

Van Gogh paints this nightmare from memory:
the virus infected fields in the flat slopes; sprawling vines
on poles; horse-drawn carts after carts; the chrome sun;
wooden baskets never filling; the hand-harvesting
throughout night where the low sun never lowers
and shadows of men drudge up the shoulders of the hills.

Rain is red on the shimmering road
and muddy areas between the vines.
The squat horizon makes him claustrophobic.
Van Gogh paints as fast as he can
while the grapes and lives ferment.

My Body Is Waiting for Gauguin
Like a Vase of Five Sunflowers

Based on paintings by Vincent van Gogh: *Self Portrait (dedicated to Paul Gauguin*, (1888), *Still Life: Vase with Five Sunflowers* (1888), and *Portrait of the Postman Joseph Roulin* (1888)

My skin is a moon torn into tiny papers.
When the bathwater speaks, I listen intently.
I do not remember how things used to be,
but it seems they are not the same.
I find myself outside of my body
and I do not have a key.

I liked things better when I do not understand them.
If I speak loudly enough, my words will fall on deaf ears.
When the door of an empty house opens,
it does not open for me.
I light a candle of darkness in a strong wind.
When you are not here, the room is a strange place
of many things speaking in hushed tones of apricots
wondering: where you are; who are the absent touches for;
why does the sky have your face;
how we can go from here when we do not want to be here.

If I knew the answers, I could bring you back to me
as a bouquet of sunflowers.

Even the mailman in the blue-sea uniform would see this.
Then he could deliver such delightful news
instead of his melancholy letters,
his dreams slipping through his pipe.

Some day the mailman will carry the news of my death
like a sea voyage.
Until then, my life is five sunflowers in a vase
waiting for some good news—
good news that you are coming.

How I Know Things Are Coming Back

Among the lupines and peonies in mid-May,
there are hidden promises of the forthcoming *Astilbe*.

What is secure this season?

Double columbines of blue geraniums,
reddish-purple tiny-leaved clematis *Etoile Violette*,
pink Japanese anemones, large white trumpets
of *'Fragrant Cloud'* solo in the chorus.
Pale white *Snow-In-Summer* spreads
on rock-edged raised beds, enjoying sunlight.

My garden is too small for my ambitions.

I have to work tight, constricted,
composing haiku of underlying colors.

If only I could've included butterscotch-gold of *Scots Pine*,
its lending of structure and intricate details,
its vessel shapes of triangular ship masts.

O what I could do with dusty-mulberry-colored *Smokebush*!

Dutchman's Breeches

(Dicentra cucullaria)

Follow a bumblebee through early Illinois spring
to tuned-down white flowers.
I'm not sure what we'll find.

Sometimes, unplanned things are best.
We could get lost, wandering like this,
in the strangeness of bee-flight.

Sometimes, we have to accept being lost
Sometimes, we see things so plainly,
yet we still don't see them.

We could get lost and simply will not care.
Perhaps, that lack of caring
is what makes it easy to find our way back.

Burrs may stick to us,
thistles rack prickles against our hands,
yet we feel no pain.

We do not care if we are far in or too far out.
Sometimes, it's best to let things just happen
in order to learn what is important.

The bees led us to the Dutchman's breeches,
in their own indirect way.
We are not in any hurry to get back.

We will return with some flowers to put in a vase
to see every aspect of them
with the eyes of bees.

Garden Haiku

hydrangeas change
between acts of a play
getting ready to perform

❧

impatiens wait
to fill the empty garden,
impatiently

❧

bees bring summer
to the creamy-peach flower
of the almond bush

❧

the radial structure
of the allium, afterwards,
spikes like frost bursts

The Bluish Butterfly Bush Calls to Me

(Buddleia davidii)

It has nectar to taste, to mash against my nose, summer spring-mist for my hair.I want to swim in it. Have its stickiness on our arms.I want to be heavy with slumber and fullness, drunk with honey, slide my tongue in like a spoon,flute it to get the most of it, and uncoil it into my belly.Then who would question if I sprouted feelers, and papery wings of symmetrical spots emerged?

If I migrated to Mexico and back,the honey locust tree I would go to next,the brutal elegance of waitingis impossible, the blossoms of musicare almost heard from behind locked white doors—the blunt wildness cannot hold me still.A pulsating moon flings fields of shaggy waters.

Gardening in Georgia Clay

I built a garden on riverbank Georgia red clay: hard dirt
used to make pottery
and not quite right for planting.

In that indeterminate soil was shale ledge, fragments
of tonsil-shaped shells, and coarse beach sand
with particles and filaments from a factory
long reduced to brick, sparkling as a night full of fireflies,

I excavated; my hands covered with shell-shocked fire ants
biting their discomfort. My hands became swollen
and inflamed for weeks, welded shut,
and almost palsied, stiff as a trowel.

I learned the hard facts: wear leather gloves
thick as determination.

The information on the seed packets
of how-to-do helped:
what conditions and starting periods
were best, when it is too late, what growing zone I was in.

After several growing seasons, after several dry seasons,
when dirt clumped into afterthoughts,
there were several on-going drenching seasons
when soil ran as rivulets taking everything with it,
including the seeds, reason, and a watering can.

A flood washed out anything I wanted to hold onto.
It was impossible to manage that red clay.

I also know about the joy of seeing the first sprout,
the warm wash of a tomato-colored sun,
sometimes, just sometimes, the impulsive clay

was enough to retain moisture,
just enough for the self-seeding *Forget-Me-Nots*
to remember what they were supposed to do.

And in those moments, I would remove the garden gloves,
head into the house, knowing what I had to do was wait.

Bloodroot

(Sanguinaria canadensis)

Those white flowers with yellow centers do not last long.
And like love, they can be gone before we know it.
The trick is to enjoy them while we can.

I would think both love
and flowers should last longer,
but I am never surprised when they do not.

Still, there are ways of prolonging love.
Say what needs to be said when in love.
Three short words open up hearts.

Enjoy the moment while it lasts.
I hope it lasts longer than I expect.
Maybe I will discover love's secret after all.

Message

The ascending flat needles on the balsam fir,
the loose, irregular, feathery needles of the hemlock,
the shaggy leaves of the cottonwood,
and the flat sprays of northern white cedar
are all I can see.

If something were to happen to me
and I was taken away from all of this,
the forest would remain
long after I was gone.

I know I will eventually go.
I hear it from the yellow warbler hanging in branches
of Lombard poplar. Its crisp music remains there,
slender in those continuous branches.

The warbler flights into tomorrow
taking news to others
they will be leaving too.

Tenderness

I want to caress a landscape, feeling the impact of the translation
of light upon the waves ingrained on a tree bark, tracing with my
fingers those deep furrowsto hear what they have seen all those
watchful years.

I crave the break of light—
a rise of startled quail; the air at sunrise;
a tree's branches, trying to hold things stilllong enough for me
to enjoy seeing them;a song of a pinfeather; a knit of string and
sprigs;or an egg holding its secrets in blue-speckled breath.Flowers
curl as earlobes do, hearing me approach, waiting for me to inspect
them for perfection, a craftsman with absolute standards.

I want to stroke across the flower's chambers,like the soft-carpeted
footstepsof an approaching lover.
In light, field sprays'skin dapples in transferred light.The flowers
have been waiting all morningfor me to kiss them with the lightest
kiss possible,not waking up or startling them, but still kiss them.

The world wants us to find all its surprises.
They blush like rose petals in the arousal of lightsliding into
awareness.

Trilliums

(Trillium grandiflorum)

His slippers scuffle across the floor.
He counts pills and vitamins, wondering
which is supposed to slow down illness.
Where did these age spots come from?
What happen to that carefree boy?
Who is that stranger in the mirror?

Ever since his body turned papery-white,
it is taking longer for him to recuperate, too.
These pills do nothing.
He has no confidence in them.
He seems to get worse as they increase in number.

The one thing he has in common with trilliums in his yard
is when they mature, they turn soft and spongy.
There is no comfort in knowing they can cure bleeding.
There is no comfort in knowing anything.

There is only comfort in finding trilliums in the springtime
opening for him
just when he needs comfort most.

Haiku Irises

the study of blue
is more than eyes can see
in colorless rain

indigo islands
swim on sea turtle shell
irises blooming

kimonos are kites
in summer brush-flutter
in my iris heart

sapphire iris
mild aperture of light
loses last petals

blue ink on woodblock
rice paper memories
pressed with irises

iris teacup broke
no fortune in tea leaves
no chipped lies either

Dogwood

IV.

Trees

Communion with the Trees

"(Trees) apostles of the living light" —Wendell Berry

We come for communion,
arriving at a place so thick with leaves
and lost light, saplings barely stand
a chance of survival.
What is cut or on fire
separates the living from the dead.
We come to make peace,
to find out what others avoid.

In this last light, one could get lost.
When that happens,
new purpose can be found, energy renewed,
all things open up and release.

This area is crowded and condensed,
compacted with pines, maples, oak, birch.
It would take a great apocalypse to cleanse it.
It needs a reaping. This is the way of recovery
and new life: the old makes way for the new.

We have come to this place
in search of the sacred and find
the healing light that filters down is not
some common light struggling
to find its way. It nurtures small, hidden
life, low to the clustered ground.

The undergrowth, full of sounds, enters our bones.

❦

We come to this untouched forest
to be in silence, to be touched by silence.
We need to hear what silence will say to us.

We do not come for benediction,
or repentance, or seeking forgiveness,
or inner peace. We come for a message.

We come for silence
among the stilled trees, far from noise
and distraction.

Sometimes, we leave empty-handed,
like branches with their leaves shaken out.

Other times, we fuse with light
and birdsong, fingers having touched ferns
and moss and dampness of silence.

Still other times, we learn once more
about the hidden secrets.

❦

Sometimes, the forest blesses.

We do not look for comfort
or companionship. Communion is
a way to talk, not necessarily out loud,
but within. We allow for an exchange,
opening to possibilities.

In thousands of Carolina wren songs
in the forest, one song is for us.
It is not too late to answer back.
We must say something worth saying.
We stand in the present
to let such music in.

Pacific Dogwood

(Cornus nuttallii)

this native species was dreadfully
scourged by disease
like his own terminal body

the straight smooth-barked
ascending branches
tipped by creamy flowers in April
often blossom again
in late summer or fall
unlike his own groaning muscles

its wood is extremely hard
pink and split-prone
it has limited and specialized uses

limited by time and age he throbs horribly

it has about twenty minuscule greenish flowers
like the diabetes dwelling unnoticed in him

each twig
is attached to a large flower
and bent to prevent
overlapping with other flowers
and there are days
when his back bends down too
carrying the weight of ages
the creaminess of cataracts form
the fall of his days that are no longer greening

From the Closeness of Oak, Dark Holds Breath

(Quercus robur)

bottomland forests at the low end
rise drenched by breathlessness
hard wood is saturated

absorbing what is given and taken
hidden small life finds sanctuary
for the temporary

survival depends on adaptability
the ecosystem supports or
it fails finding or losing a connection

insects carry seeds under a thicket of leaves
some accidental planting happens
hundreds of butterflies burst out into light

their silence has been accumulating
like blue herons becoming cumulous clouds
breathless as the land finding bottom

Song of Loneliness

Box Elder (*Acer negundo*)

The box elder wrestles the wind,
the damp nights, the stars
grazing the meadows of the endless horizon,
the snow creeping up, the frost's
speckled finger markings.

I wish I could tolerate the winter,
but I have to go inside,
check the thermostat a couple of times,
wrap a comforter around my shoulders,
shiver out the deep chill,
while the wind whines, a child
waking with night terrors.

I know the song of loneliness when I hear it.

That music settles in differently
than my body trying to generate heat.
Each recollection, each storage
of lost body heat co-mingles with branches
in fierce wind, shuddering. Each star
vaguely behind cold
meadows of clouds, snow sneaking in,
offers no comfort, no solace,
no rest from nightmares,
no matter how tightly I grip the blanket,
no matter what song I sing to myself
to keep the sadness from entering me,
a deep and sullen chill.

Divinization

In Norse mythology, Odin hung himself on
an ash tree for nine days to learn the runes.

I have cut some branches
from the only fruit-bearing tree in the ice forest
and carved on its spines secret meanings known only to me.
A secret well-kept is like a sharp two-headed axe.
A man who can hold his own breath in his hands in the winter
can always find the source of the sun frozen in the sky.

I scatter these fragments of scrawled branches onto a white cloth,
white as the forever landscape,
white as my beard when ice forms on its edge.
A secret shared brings new enemies.
A man should do everything to keep to himself
when he cannot see anything.

I close my frostbit eyes for a moment before lifting my head
and staring into the face of the Frost Gods.
Now, I can interpret these three pieces of wood
like they were a woman under white skins calling me to come.
A secret whispered into a woman's ear always causes laughter
like the tingle of icicles. A man can only hold so many things.

I can see the clear path in front of me, even in this endless darkness.
A secret is a world of snow devouring your footsteps
so that no one can follow. A man who keeps life simple and familiar
will always be able to read runes, for each rune casting
and each interpretation is as individual as each man.

Druid Astrology Is Written in the Trees

I. Birch: The Achiever
    December 24–January 20

    Because we are born in darkness,
    we search for light—
    this is the greatest ambition.
    We are always reaching for more.
    More is never enough.

    A birch adapts to harsh environments, being tough
    when it needs to be, and resilient
    when all others fail.

    Its sign makes us cool-headed in conflict,
    aware of our gentler side;
    even a barren land
    improves by our presence.

    Light always arrives where it is needed most.

II. Rowan: The Thinker
    January 21–February 17

    We cannot control the urge to share ideas,
    for what we see
    is not clear to others.
    Words get in the way.

    Waxwings eat rowan red berries all winter,
    thinking of better food in spring.

We make our way through life the best we can
with whatever we are given—
some find more, and some find less.

III.   Ash: The Enchanter
       February 18–March 17

The white ash's thick, scaly,
diamond-patterned bark
is darkroom black—

intuition—
knowing something is coming
in continuous renewal.

This sign is inspired by nature,
constantly thinking—
then we are onto the next object we see.

Imagination is renewing the self,
healing the moody and withdrawn artist,
or driving them deeper into loss.

We've been hiding all winter.
Now, it is time to emerge like a bear
before everyone concludes we are recluses.

But we have been composing like poems,
revising darkness into couplets,
touching air to feel its colors.

The land is constantly shifting for us.
Everything is in motion or it is too stiff
and unyielding,

even the early shoots,

Johnny-jump-ups, are too sudden,
yet reassuring.

IV.   Alder: The Trailblazer
      March 18–April 14

      Its red catkins draw butterflies
      while the tree itself creates
      a symbiotic relationship with the soil.

      This sign is all action and results.
      Everyone wants to be our friend.
      Confidence is combustible.
      Our belief in ourselves is infectious,
      rubbing off on everyone.
      We are as focused as rain in April.

V.   Willow: The Observer
      April 15–May 12

      The moon is our sign.
      It is that cross-hatching in the web of our palms.
      We are many hands in the mystic world,
      knowing what will happen
      before it happens. We want to know the cycles,
      the inheritance of being psychic.
      Perspective depends on which way we face the moon.
      Memory is a pool we drink, endlessly.

      Ancient fishing nets were made from a willow.

      A willow is used by healers for aches
      and fevers, known by Hippocrates,
      Native Americans, and druids.

It's now used in aspirin.
This is old knowledge for new medicines.

My wife weaves a basket from willows
to hold all the knowledge of the world.
She interweaves part intelligence and part-
seasons, always connected, always
old and new, always potentially
waiting for someone to open the lid,
let the winds take them
to whoever receives them
with open, welcoming arms.

VI.   Hawthorn: The Illusionist
May 13–June 9

Nothing is what it appears to be.
The surface holds something different inside
just like the hawthorn
whose fruit looks like plum stones
and is tart and red like crabapples,
food for nectar-feeding insects,
made into Mexican jams
for pre-Christmas celebration
Los Posadas, or known as Zalzalak
in Iran and eaten raw,
or dried and used in Chinese medicines
for digestion problems.

And although its thorn-sharp branches
are believed to be the crown for Christ,
its leaves are edible in salads,

its white flowers
used in druid weddings
as an emblem of hope,

its branches used
to heal a broken heart in Ireland,
or deadly to vampires in Serbia.

The tree marks the entrance
to the Otherworld for early Scots,
found close to holy wells
with healing rags tied to branches.

This sign is the excellent listener,
able to see the big picture
and all the components.
Our observations can comfort some,
or increase worry for others.
What we do with our insights
is out of our hands, released like crows
from the ark in search of solid land,
finding illusion and more searching.

VII.   Oak: The Stabilizer
June 10–July 7

Our sign is the protector. We are strength
when someone needs it, comfort for seekers,
a voice for those who cannot speak for themselves,
supporting the weak, generous with what we have,
helpful when others were not.
We always assume everything will work out—
it seldom does. Structure is important.
Study history and ancestry like some people study
bird flight or river currents or moon phases.

Perhaps it is because the oak is insect resistant,
that it was hewed into Viking ships,
floors, barrels for whiskey, or tanning leather.

The willingness to impart wisdom
means we will become teachers.

VIII.   Holly: The Ruler
        July 8 –August 4

We overcome obstacles with skill and tact.
For us, there are no set-backs.
Our vigilance will not allow any,
keeping a watchful eye. We do not let
our natural competitive nature
get in our way. We are our own worst enemy.
Do not become arrogant;
no one likes that side of us.

The holly has the red decorative berry,
but its wood was used for bagpipes.
Druids wore its laurel branches on their heads
as a symbol of truth.

If we are not careful, we can slip,
become lazy, off-balance,
undependable. For everything positive,
there is a negative lurking somewhere
making it impossible to obtain our goals.

IX.   Hazel: The Knower
        August 5–September 1

What we know today might not be true tomorrow.
Organized and efficient, able to recall

with a photographic memory,
we can appear as know-it-alls.

We know the best course of action—
abandon our unchecked compulsions.
There is such a thing as too much of a good thing.

Remember, the hazel nut is hard outside,
but soft inside. Knowing the self is important.

According to legend, the hazel dropped nuts
into a sacred pool, a salmon swallowed one
gaining wisdom. A teacher, wanting to be all-knowing,
told his student to catch that salmon, cook it,
but never eat it. In the process of cooking,
hot water splashed on the student's thumb;
he sucked on it to cool it, accidentally
obtaining the fish's wisdom, becoming
the Druid hero, Finn McCool.

Our sign swims with memory.

X. Vine: The Equalizer
    September 2–September 29

The autumnal equinox is changeable
and unpredictable. Contradiction is our name.
We can see both sides of any story,
but we are not sure of anything.
Everything we touch is not golden.

Remember: vines are clingy,
attaching to anything
and entangling everything in their way.

Do not be sure of everything;
appearances change too radically.

XI.   Ivy: The Survivor
      September 30–October 27

Born in a time of a waning sun,
life can be difficult at times.
It seems so unfair, doesn't it?
Who will be there to lend a helping hand?
Obstacles are coming faster than we can adapt.
These are troubling times.
This calls for a spiritual centering,
clinging to what is good and familiar.
We must persevere.
We are better than any adversity.

Ivy keeps low to the ground, creeping
over obstacles, climbing over anything
in the way, clutching to outcrops.
Its greenish-yellow flowers have nectar;
its roots can lance brick walls
and break them. This is our sign.

XII.   Reed: The Inquisitor
      October 28–November 24

We keep secrets.
We know how to find the hidden meanings.
We know the layers to the heart.
We could be a journalist, historian, detective,
archeologist, always digging,
no matter where it takes us.
The harvest is behind us. The climate is harsh
and unknown. We know how to interpret,
but do we know what to say?

Reeds were sacred to the druids for pipes before war
or funerals. Both manipulate death.
Both know scheming. Both know coaxing
and the pathway to the next life.

Our sign knows the diversity of meaning,
the separate paths all truths must take
in order to meet.

Beneath the layers of stories, we hear
there is some overlapping reality
by all the speakers.
We must choose which story is
the correct story
like a judge without evidence
except hearsay and innuendo.

Be careful not to manipulate the evidence.
Scheming is seldom harmless.

XIII. Elder: The Seeker
       November 25–December 23

       Now is the time for wildness,
       to speed things up, to live
       like there is no tomorrow,
       discovering everything—

       we act irrationally
       because the sun is less each day
       and we have to fit everything in

       in the shortest amount of time possible
       before we run out of time.

Time is our worst enemy;
but so is impatience.

Black elderberry has been used to cure flues,
allergies, and respiratory diseases.
What can cure us?

When the world seems darker, remember:
light always returns.

MARTIN WILLITTS JR. is a Quaker. He is a retired Librarian and musician living in Syracuse, New York. He is an editor for *The Comstock Review* and a judge for the New York State Fair Poetry Contest.

He has been nominated for seventeen Pushcart and thirteen Best of the Net awards. Winner of the 2012 Big River Poetry Review's William K. Hathaway Award; 2013 Bill Holm Witness Poetry Contest; 2013 "Trees" Poetry Contest; 2014 Broadsided Award; 2014 Dylan Thomas International Poetry Contest; *Rattle* Ekphrastic Challenge, June 2015, Editor's Choice; *Rattle* Ekphrastic Challenge, Artist's Choice, November 2016, Stephen A. DiBiase Poetry Prize, 2018; *Rattle* Ekphrastic Challenge, Editor's Choice, December, 2020.

photo: Linda Griggs

His twenty-four chapbooks include National Chapbook Contest winner *William Blake, Not Blessed Angel but Restless Man* (Red Ochre Press, 2014) and Turtle Island Editor's Choice Award *The Wire Fence Holding Back the World* (Flowstone Press, 2016).

His twenty-two full-length books include National Ecological Award winner *Searching for What You Cannot See* (Hiraeth Press, 2013); *How to Be Silent* (FutureCycle Press, 2016); *Dylan Thomas and the Writer's Shed* (FutureCycle Press, 2017); *Three Ages of Women* (Deerbrook Editions, 2017); *Home Coming Celebration* (FutureCycle Press, 2019); 2019 Blue Light Award winner *The Temporary World*; *Unfolding of Love* (Wipf and Stock Publishers, 2020); *Harvest Time* (Deerbrook Press, 2021).

SHANTI ARTS

NATURE · ART · SPIRIT

Please visit us online
to browse our entire book catalog,
including poetry collections and fiction,
books on travel, nature, healing, art,
photography, and more.

Also take a look at our highly regarded art
and literary journal, *Still Point Arts Quarterly*,
which may be downloaded for free.

www.shantiarts.com